Negotiation Basics

Win-Win Strategies for Everyone

Fourth Edition

Charles P. Lickson J.D., Ph.D. and Robert B. Maddux

A Crisp Fifty-Minute™ Series Book

This Fifty-Minute™ Book is designed to be "read with a pencil." It is an excellent workbook for self-study as well as classroom learning. All material is copyright-protected and cannot be duplicated without permission from the publisher. *Therefore, be sure to order a copy for every training participant by contacting:*

1-800-442-7477 ◆ 25 Thomson Place, Boston, MA ◆ www.courseilt.com

Negotiation Basics
Win-Win Strategies for Everyone

Fourth Edition

Charles P. Lickson J.D., Ph.D. and Robert B. Maddux

CREDITS:

Production Manager:	**Debbie Woodbury**
Editor:	**Marguerite Langlois**
Production Editor:	**Genevieve McDermott**
Production Artists:	**Nicole Phillips, Rich Lehl, and Betty Hopkins**
Production Team:	**Denise Powers and Melissa Hulse**

For more information contact:

NETg
25 Thomson Place
Boston, MA 02210

Or find us on the Web at **www.courseilt.com**

For permission to use material from this text or product, submit a request online at: www.thomsonrights.com

Any additional questions about permissions can be submitted by e-mail to: thomsonrights@thomson.com

Trademarks

Crisp Fifty-Minute Series is a trademark of NETg.

Some of the product names and company names used in this book have been used for identification purposes only and may be trademarks or registered trademarks of their respective manufacturers and sellers.

Disclaimer

NETg reserves the right to revise this publication and make changes from time to time in its content without notice.

ISBN 0-619-25907-8
Library of Congress Catalog Card Number 2005925072
Printed in the United States of America
2 3 4 5 GP 08 07 06

Learning Objectives for

NEGOTIATION BASICS

The learning objectives for *Negotiation Basics* are listed below. They have been developed to guide the user to the core issues covered in this book.

The objectives of this book are to help the user:

1) Explore negotiation opportunities and approaches

2) Understand the steps necessary for negotiations to work effectively

3) Learn negotiation strategies and tactics for success

4) Understand negotiation skills using the case study method

5) Find resources for further information on and support for negotiation

Assessing Progress

NETg has developed a Crisp Series **assessment** that covers the fundamental information presented in this book. A 25-item, multiple-choice and true/false questionnaire allows the reader to evaluate his or her comprehension of the subject matter. To buy the assessment and answer key, go to www.courseilt.com and search on the book title or via the assessment format, or call 1-800-442-7477.

Assessments should not be used in any employee-selection process.

About the Author

Charles P. Lickson is a former corporate and trial attorney-turned-professional mediator. He received his traditional training at Johns Hopkins University (B.A. with political science honors) and Georgetown Law Center (J.D.). He also holds a non-traditional Ph.D. in counseling.

Dr. Lickson is the author of six books, including *Legal Guide for Small Business, Ethics for Government Employees, Finance and Taxes for the Home-Based Business* (with co-author Bryane Miller Lickson), and *Ironing It Out: Seven Simple Steps to Resolving Conflict* (each published by Crisp Publications).

In addition to being a Virginia Supreme Court certified mediator, Dr. Lickson is a qualified arbitrator and facilitator and a founding member and Fellow of the International Academy of Mediators. He is an adjunct associate professor of political science and public administration at Shenandoah University in Winchester, Virginia, where he teaches courses in conflict resolution, political science, and ethics. And he is a senior neutral and trainer at the Conflict Management Consortium, Inc., Front Royal, Virginia.

Dr. Lickson has led many training programs in basic and advanced negotiation skills and in conflict resolution. He has been involved in resolving over 1,500 cases of varying types with a recent emphasis on family, organizational, and workplace disputes.

Preface

Negotiation is often thought of as a contest in which one side wins and the other side loses. Many books, articles, and tapes tout "swim with the sharks," "negotiate to win," "guerilla negotiation," and other "I win—you lose" concepts.

The truth is that we negotiate every day with a view toward meeting our needs without antagonizing or defeating others. This kind of negotiating is known as *win-win* or *collaborative* problem solving. Such win-win negotiation has been proven to be far more effective in getting results without costly emotional and financial outcomes. It also helps to preserve relationships. After many years negotiating for myself and on behalf of clients, my own career has led me away from so-called traditional, adversarial negotiating to a more collaborative non-traditional approach.

This book is a revision of the Crisp bestseller, *Successful Negotiation,* by the late Robert B. Maddux. The new title, *Negotiation Basics: Win-Win Strategies for Everyone,* reflects more clearly what you can expect from this book: the basics you need to begin practicing successful negotiation skills whenever you need them.

This book looks at all forms of negotiating, but emphasizes win-win negotiating principles and strategies. It includes new concepts, tools, and guidance, reflecting recent advances in collaboration and cooperation and new attitudes toward negotiation. The book also draws upon my own book *Ironing It Out: Seven Simple Steps to Resolving Conflict,* also published by Crisp, and my many years of practical negotiation experience as an attorney, businessperson, counselor, and professional mediator.

By following the simple steps in this book and learning the basics of *interest-based (win-win) bargaining* described here, you can get what you need without giving in or risking harm to delicate relationships. You will also learn what to do when nothing seems to work. Read on—and put these tools to good use in your work and personal life.

Charles P. Lickson

This edition is dedicated to the memory of Robert B. Maddux.

Table of Contents

PART 1

An Introduction

to Negotiation

What Is Negotiation?

> *" We spend a great deal of time negotiating...most managers and supervisors spend up to 50% of their time negotiating. The outcomes of these negotiations determine our success in both our professional and personal lives. "*

> **–Brad McRae,** *Negotiating and Influencing Skills*

You are about to embark on a brief study of the principles of negotiation. You are already negotiating every day, and you already have an interest, or you wouldn't be reading this book. You probably want to learn more about negotiation or how to become more proficient as a negotiator. Let's start by comparing some of your ideas with those of the author.

Your Ideas

We negotiate at home, we negotiate at work, we negotiate in other aspects of our lives. Most of the time we are negotiating to get something we want. Sometimes, we are negotiating to rid ourselves of what we don't want. As you begin this study of negotiation, take a few minutes to look at your own thoughts.

1. In the space below, write what the word *negotiation* means to you.

   _____

   _____

2. What, in your view, prompts negotiation among companies, groups, and/or individuals?

   _____

   _____

3. How frequently do you think most people negotiate?

   ❑ Very rarely

   ❑ Almost every day

   ❑ A few times each year

Negotiation—Some Practical Definitions

The *American Heritage Desk Dictionary* defines *negotiation* as "conferring with another in order to come to terms or reach an agreement."

Here are some other ways to think about negotiation:

➤ Negotiation is, simply stated, formalized discussion between two parties or organizations.

➤ Negotiation refers to the process we use to satisfy our needs when someone else controls what we are seeking. Other words sometimes used to describe negotiation are: bargaining, exchanging, and haggling.

➤ Negotiation has traditionally been thought of as the process of attempting to satisfy your wants, by giving up something you now have in exchange for something else you want.

➤ Negotiation and conflict are closely related. Sometimes we negotiate to avoid conflict. Other times, we use negotiation to resolve conflict.

➤ Negotiation applies to everyday exchanges in business or personal life where agreement is reached over buying and selling, exchanging services or property, resolving differences, or engaging in mutually desirable projects. There are many examples, from such simple tasks as deciding with colleagues where to have lunch to such complex issues as discussing with a builder the cost of constructing a new home.

How did your ideas about negotiation compare with these? Perhaps these descriptions gave you some new ideas about negotiation. We'll be exploring these ideas throughout this book.

One thing is certain about negotiation—we each do it every day! Some of us are better at it than others, and we get more of what we seek. Sometimes we can be negotiating without even knowing it. But negotiation results are better when we know that is what we are doing. Thus, understanding what negotiation is and how it works, and being prepared to negotiate should lead us to a better result.

It is okay to negotiate!

Identifying Opportunities for Negotiation

Now that we have a sense of what negotiation is, let's look next at when to negotiate.

Many people miss the opportunity to make a more favorable exchange because they fail to recognize the opportunity to negotiate. But any aspect of a transaction that is not totally satisfactory to you is worth negotiating.

Are You Missing Opportunities for Negotiation?

Here is a list of the kinds of transactions we might face in our own lives. Please check (✓) those that you think offer an opportunity to improve your position through the process of negotiation.

- ❑ 1. Purchasing a new car
- ❑ 2. Deciding with the family where to vacation this year
- ❑ 3. Getting a raise in pay
- ❑ 4. Selecting a dress for the senior prom
- ❑ 5. Meeting with an employee group over work rules
- ❑ 6. Deciding on a new product to launch
- ❑ 7. Agreeing on new curtains for the dining room
- ❑ 8. Buying new furniture for the office
- ❑ 9. Deciding who gets to use the family computer each evening
- ❑ 10. Agreeing on the terms of a new business loan

What other areas in your work or personal life involve negotiating?

_____

_____

_____

As you may have guessed by now, all of the above situations could involve negotiating. Some are more challenging than others. Some require serious thought and planning. Others can flow quickly and easily. Read on and be prepared to deepen your understanding of negotiation and to sharpen your skills as a negotiator.

Are you prepared to handle these situations effectively?

To Negotiate or Not—That Is the Question

Quick reactions to situations, especially conflict, rarely involve negotiation. They may involve discussion, emotion, upset, even argument, but not negotiation. Before looking at how to negotiate, we must first ask ourselves if negotiation is the best choice or most appropriate under the circumstances.

Negotiation can only happen when there is time to do it and when there is a purpose or something you can accomplish. So, there will be occasions where there is either no time, or no purpose achieved by engaging in the process of negotiation.

We've seen that opportunities to negotiate occur in many personal interactions, but sometimes you don't want to negotiate, or should not do so. The following are two examples:

➤ Your child runs into the street and you fear for her life. Are you going to negotiate her return to the sidewalk? No way! You are going to get her out of the street as quickly as possible using any means, verbal or otherwise, to accomplish that goal.

➤ Let's say you have agreed at work to put in extra hours for no extra pay because of the financial condition of the firm. Your gallant efforts have helped, but your boss seeks to add one more hour a day without pay. You are already stretched thin with home and financial responsibilities. Are you going to negotiate that extra non-paid hour? Maybe, maybe not.

Negotiation and Conflict

"*A basic fact about negotiation…is that you are dealing not with abstract representatives of the other side, but with human beings.*"

–Fisher, Ury, and Patton, *Getting To Yes*

Conflict and negotiation often go hand in hand. Sometimes the negotiation happens first and the conflict arises out of an unsuccessful negotiation. Other times the conflict leads to negotiation to resolve the differences and eliminate the conflict.

As you will soon see, successful negotiators have a positive attitude. They can view conflict as normal and constructive. The skills they use to resolve conflict are not "magic." They can be learned. Learning these skills can give you the courage and confidence necessary to challenge others, and to initiate a positive negotiation. Understanding the skills of negotiation also sustains you when others challenge you.

What Is Your Attitude Toward Negotiation?

As we begin our study of negotiation, check your attitude toward negotiation, disagreement, and conflict by reading the statements below and thinking about how accurately (or not) each statement describes you. The number five indicates that the statement applies most strongly to you.

	Strong Agreement			Mild Agreement	
It doesn't bother me to question a price asked for something or to seek a more favorable exchange than the one offered.	5	4	3	2	1
I have nothing to lose in seeking a better deal if I do it in a reasonable way.	5	4	3	2	1
Conflict is a fact of life.	5	4	3	2	1
When I am in conflict, I work hard to resolve it.	5	4	3	2	1
Conflict is positive because it makes me examine my ideas carefully.	5	4	3	2	1
In resolving conflict, I try to consider the needs of the other person; in fact, I believe conflict often produces better solutions to problems.	5	4	3	2	1
I don't mind conflict. In fact, conflict stimulates my thinking and sharpens my judgment.	5	4	3	2	1
Working with conflict has taught me that compromise is not necessarily a sign of weakness.	5	4	3	2	1
Satisfactorily resolved, conflict often strengthens relationships.	5	4	3	2	1
Conflict is a way to test one's own point of view.	5	4	3	2	1

Grand Total _____

If most of the statements reflected your thinking, you have a realistic attitude toward conflict and seem willing to work to resolve it. If you identified with more than half of the statements, you appear to be dealing fairly well with conflict, but need to work toward a more positive approach.

If you agreed with fewer than half of the sentences, you need to first understand why and then work hard to learn the techniques of conflict resolution.[*] By the time you finish this book, you may wish to complete this exercise again.

---

[*] For excellent insights into resolving conflict, read *Managing Disagreement Constructively,* by Herbert S. Kindler Ph.D., and *Ironing It Out: Seven Simple Steps to Resolving Conflict,* by Charles P. Lickson J.D., Ph.D. Both are Crisp Series books by Thomson Learning.

Understanding Types of Negotiation

To simplify looking at types of negotiation, we can look at the environment, the urgency, or need for the negotiation, as well as the personal approach or style of the negotiators.

Looking at it from this perspective, we can categorize negotiation into five principle types:

➤ Everyday (Or Casual) Negotiations

➤ Informal Negotiations

➤ Formal Negotiations

➤ Facilitated Negotiations

➤ Critical Negotiations

Let's look at each of these types in more detail.

Everyday Negotiations

We already know that every day, in communicating about our wants and needs or engaging in minor problem solving, we conduct casual negotiations. Here is an example:

Sylvia's Internship: An Everyday or Casual Negotiation

Sylvia was finishing college. During the summer between her junior and senior year at State U, she served as an intern in the marketing department of Widget International ("Widget"). Her boss and mentor was Alice Jones. Sylvia didn't understand much about working in an organization. A number of times that summer, Alice and Sylvia had relaxed conversations about how things were done at Widget and what Sylvia was expected to do. Several times Sylvia needed time off to do research on a paper due in the fall. She and Alice easily worked out the details and both women felt fine about the arrangement.

Now think of an example of an everyday negotiation you have been in or have witnessed and note it here.

Informal Negotiations

Sometimes we make it clear to the other party that we expect to engage in a more serious conversation toward resolving some problem or obtaining something we want from that party. Most of these conversations take place in an informal environment.

Sylvia's Vacation: An Informal Negotiation

At one point late in the summer of her internship, Sylvia's parents asked her to accompany them to the beach for a week-long vacation. Sylvia went to her supervisor, Alice, with the request. Alice explained that an important project was scheduled for that week and Sylvia's help was needed. Sylvia expressed her desire to help out at Widget, but also explained that this might be the last opportunity she would have to vacation with her parents.

After some serious discussion in an informal environment, Alice and Sylvia worked out a plan. Sylvia and her parents would each take their own car to the beach, and Sylvia would return to work on Wednesday of the big project week.

Now think of an example of an informal negotiation you have been in or have witnessed and note it here.

_____

Formal Negotiations

On occasion it is necessary to discuss issues on a more formalized basis. These negotiations are usually planned in advance. They follow set agendas and may even require representatives, such as a lawyer or union rep, to be present to assist in the discussions. Also, more formal negotiations may take place in a neutral location and be of longer duration. These discussions can continue over periods of days or weeks—even months or longer.

Sylvia Goes to Work: A Formal Negotiation

After graduation from State U with excellent grades, Sylvia applies for a job at Widget. The company is very interested in her, especially because of the kind things Alice had to say about the quality of Sylvia's work and her dedication to her responsibilities at the company when she was an intern.

Richard, Vice President of Marketing (Alice's boss) interviews Sylvia with a view toward hiring her as a Marketing Assistant. He offers her a very minimal salary with a review at the end of one year, followed by a possible raise.

Sylvia is well prepared for her meeting with Richard. She has documented the tasks she accomplished for Widget while an intern the previous summer.

Richard responds that there is great competition for the job Sylvia wants.

Sylvia points out, most respectfully, that she knows Alice wants her and none of the other candidates.

After several friendly, but serious, interchanges, Richard offers Sylvia a job at a somewhat higher salary, with a review at the end of six months toward a possible raise.

Sylvia accepts. She begins working at Widget, on staff, the following Monday.

Now think of an example of a formal negotiation you have been in or have witnessed and note it here.

_____

Facilitated Negotiations

Sometimes, the assistance of a neutral or impartial third party is necessary to help parties negotiate to agreement. The third party, the person who assists, is limited to facilitating agreement between the negotiators. These "facilitated negotiations" are also referred to as mediation. The mediator acts to empower the negotiating parties to reach their own resolution. The mediator does not have a vote in the outcome. [Note: Sometimes mediation is confused with arbitration. They are both methods of resolving conflict in a nontraditional way (what lawyers refer to as "alternative dispute resolution" or "ADR") However, in arbitration the third party makes the decision. Arbitration, therefore, is not a negotiation. As noted above, in mediation, the parties make the decision themselves.] The negotiated agreement belongs to the parties themselves—even if they have received the assistance of a third party acting as mediator.

Sylvia Needs Assistance: A Facilitated Negotiation

Sylvia is very happy at work; however, she is not getting along well with Tom, a co-worker in the Marketing Department. She has tried talking to Tom about the problem, but Tom refuses to respond. Finally, Sylvia asks Alice if she can assist Sylvia and Tom in resolving their differences.

Alice approaches Tom about a meeting with Sylvia and herself. Tom agrees. The three meet in Alice's office. Alice asks each to explain what is going on. Tom explains that he resents Sylvia getting a reserved parking place after being at work only 7 months, while, he has worked 5 years without a designated space. Sylvia explains that she didn't ask for the space and doesn't even need it. Tom did not know that Sylvia never asked for the space. Sylvia says she is happy to give up the space and Tom could have it if she wanted it. Tom says he really doesn't need it either, but feels better now knowing that Sylvia hadn't asked for it and was willing to give it to him.

Both Sylvia and Tom shake hands and thank Alice for her assistance in resolving the issue that had come between them at work. Alice acknowledges Tom and Sylvia's willingness to be open about what was bothering them. Soon, all three are back at work.

Now think of an example of a facilitated negotiation (mediation) you have been in or have witnessed and note it here.

Critical Negotiations

Sometimes, but rarely, discussions take place on an emergency basis with serious possible consequences for failure. These kinds of critical negotiations often involve an outside intervener, such as a pastor, police officer, or mental health worker. Negotiations undertaken during war, national emergency, or crisis are, by virtue of the situation under which the negotiations take place, critical. It is important to note that even in such situations, negotiations can occur. Let's look next at a critical negotiation which takes place at Sylvia's workplace.

Sylvia Witnesses a Crisis: A Critical Negotiation

One day, after Sylvia has been working at Widget for a year, an announcement comes over the company public address system for all employees to leave the West Building immediately. Sylvia wonders what is going on. She and other employees heard police sirens and witnessed much activity outside the East Building.

Richard rushes into Alice's office, where Sylvia is now working, and tells Alice, Sylvia, and their secretary to get out of the building fast. He alerts other members of the Marketing staff to vacate the building immediately through the nearest exit, but not to go near the East Building.

Once outside in the parking lot behind the West Building, Sylvia and other staffers learn that an upset former employee has taken the company president and his office staff hostage on the top floor of the East Building.

After Sylvia and her colleagues have been standing around nervously for about 30 minutes, a police captain comes to the parking lot to announce that the crisis is over. The hostage negotiator convinced the former employee to surrender and free all hostages. No one was hurt. According to the police captain, it was the negotiator's skill in dealing with critical issues for the hostage taker which prevented a tragedy.

Richard thanked the captain for the good news and informed Sylvia and the other junior staffers to take the rest of the day off.

Now think of an example of a critical negotiation you have been in or have witnessed and note it here.

Fortunately, critical negotiations are the rarest. In fact, most negotiations in our lives will be of the everyday or informal types. When we negotiate things like a major purchase, employment agreement, or bank loan, the negotiation becomes more formalized.

All types of negotiation, however, have similar characteristics and common steps in the process. They all have potential for success or failure depending on how effectively the negotiation is undertaken.

Summary

Here is a list of the main concepts covered in this part. Check the ones that are most important to you.

- ❑ Negotiation is a process we use to get what we want or need when someone else has what we are seeking.

- ❑ Negotiation is part of everyday life.

- ❑ We choose whether or not to negotiate, and when and where to negotiate, according to the particular situation we are in.

- ❑ Conflict goes hand-in-hand with negotiation, and our attitudes toward conflict make a difference in how we negotiate.

- ❑ We can learn specific skills that will help us to negotiate effectively.

P A R T 2

Negotiation: Attitudes and Approaches

Negotiation Styles

" *Once the negotiation is over, both sides, especially the people directly involved, have to live with the agreement."*

–**Morrison and Calero,** *The Human Side of Negotiation*

When you think of "negotiation," do you see it as a way to get something (a process) or as a thing itself (an object) in other words—a verb or a noun?

It has been said that negotiations should be seen as a beginning, not as an end. Since negotiation is really a method to obtain something you want or need, and since you may very well have to interact with the other side in the future, the "scorched earth" (i.e., "winner take all") approach is not too wise. You want to aim at styles and approaches to negotiation that are effective for both the short term and the long term. This is particularly important when you are negotiating with people you spend a lot of time with, such as at home or at work.

Negotiation styles relate to how people deal with conflict. The following are the generally accepted negotiation styles or attitudes most people use when confronting conflict or opposition:

➤ Forcing/Adversarial (Win/Lose)

➤ Accommodating (Lose/Win)

➤ Compromising (Give/ Get)

➤ Collaborative /Non-Adversarial (Win/Win)

Negotiation styles have a direct bearing on the attitude or approach you will take to the negotiation. If your personal negotiation style is along the lines of "I must win," you fall into the *forcing* model. Perhaps you feel it is better in the negotiation to just give in. Then, you fall into the *accommodating* negotiation style. If you sincerely feel that in order to get what you want in the negotiation you must give up something, you are in the *compromising* style. And, if your approach is problem-solving, aiming at both parties winning, you are using the *collaborative* style.

There is no magic to any of these styles. Sometimes you may feel the need to be forceful, or compromising, or accommodating. In most situations, however, you will find that the collaborative style has the greatest chance for success.

Primary Motivational Value System

According to the Relationship Awareness® theory approach to human behavior, each of us has a primary motivational value system—the way we relate to others in the world when things are going well for us. The late Dr. Elias Porter, a renowned clinical psychologist, described people as motivated by altruistic, assertive, or data-oriented styles. He also recognized there could be blends, and a style made up of equal portions of the three. This motivational value system will likely change when we find ourselves in conflict or opposition. Dr. Porter concluded that people do what they do because they want to feel good about themselves.[*]

Assuming that you do what you do in order to feel good about yourself, the truth is, you bring who you are and what you value to the negotiation. While you may adopt an aggressive, moderate, submissive, or cooperative persona during the process, you will meet your goals only when you are clear on what you want and why you want it.

Thus, your approach to negotiating will reflect:

➤ Who you are

➤ What it will take in the negotiation to make you feel good about yourself

Attitude will affect your approach to anything. Attitude is always important, and this is especially true in negotiating. Attitudes influence our objectives, objectives control the way we negotiate, and the way in which we negotiate affects the outcome.

Attitude → Approach → Objectives → Negotiation Style → Outcome

How do you think about your objectives when you negotiate? Have you considered those of the other party? Can you both win? The exercise on the following page will give you some insights into your attitude and thus, your negotiating style.

---

[*] Relationship Awareness® theory is a registered trademark of Personal Strengths Publishing, Inc., Carlsbad, California and is used here with permission.

EVALUATING YOUR ATTITUDE

Let's take a look at your potential attitude toward negotiating. In this self-evaluation, place a check (✓) by the statements that come closest to your thoughts about negotiation.

1. By and large, I see myself in day-to-day activities as:

   ❑ A. Willing to pursue vigorously what I want in order to get it

   ❑ B. Willing to give in to avoid conflict or confrontation

   ❑ C. Willing to compromise or give in to get what I can

   ❑ D. Willing to collaborate to see how both sides can come away with a sense of achievement

2. With regard to seeking a particular goal, I would:

   ❑ A. Not stop until I get it, if possible

   ❑ B. Stop in order to avoid upsetting myself or others

   ❑ C. Find a way of getting something, even if not the whole thing

   ❑ D. Try to find out what the other person wants and see if we can both win

3. Once the discussion/negotiation is over, I would:

   ❑ A. Do what I thought was right, even if it didn't live up to the exact terms of the negotiated result

   ❑ B. Do anything I could to avoid being accused of not living up to the agreement

   ❑ C. Try to change any part of the agreement I didn't like by finding something else to give the other side

   ❑ D. Do my best to live up to it, and if I was having difficulty with any part of it, would approach the other side to try to find a mutual solution

Obviously, this brief self-evaluation is not an in-depth psychological test or personal profile; however, it can help you see the way you approach discussions and negotiations.

CONTINUED

If most of your answers were (B), you don't like conflict and would do almost anything to avoid it. This style is sometimes referred to as accommodating.

If most of your answers were (C), compromise would be your approach of choice. You are comfortable giving in, in part, as long as you can get something in return.

If most of your answers were (D), you like to find the common ground wherever possible. This is the collaborative (problem-solving) style. People with the collaborative approach automatically ask, "How can we both win?" Having both sides win usually means that interests or needs are being satisfied. This approach, where the attention is focused on finding common ground, is sometimes called *interest-based bargaining*.

While there are no correct answers to this self-evaluation, you can draw some interesting observations and conclusions about approaching negotiation. Studies have shown that the most successful negotiations fall into the collaborative style.

If your own approach is different, think about how you might adopt a more collaborative or win-win approach.

The Win-Win Approach to Negotiation

> "*Experimental studies and case studies suggest that people with collaborative negotiation training obtain better outcomes than those without such training.*"

—Lum and Wanis-St. John, *A New ICON for Negotiation Advice*

If we are to engage in the collaborative approach—interest-based bargaining—to reach win-win outcomes, we need to understand what we mean by the term interests when we talk about negotiation, and why that is important.

Meeting High-Priority Needs

People tend to understand the term "interests" in the context of what they feel is important to them. That's the way we will use the word here: interests usually represent people's needs as opposed to their wants.

People are persistent about having their needs (i.e. their interests) met and will probably be less flexible about these. Needs represent things people feel they *must* have vs. things they feel they'd *like* to have.

Most negotiations are successful when parties' high-priority needs and interests are satisfied—even if not all their needs are met. However, if none of their needs can be met, you can be assured the negotiation probably won't succeed, unless the other party is an accommodator using giving in to achieve his own goals.

Finding Common Ground

A common perception of negotiation is that it represents a contest. Most contests have winners and losers. The concept of interest-based bargaining is designed to focus the discussion on finding common ground and on both parties' needs. This directs the discussion away from win/lose toward win/win. In resolving conflict, finding the best options for mutual success inevitably proves most effective.

Since the 1980s, much valuable work has been done on developing win-win approaches to negotiation and conflict resolution. Much of the credit for this more current and successful attitude toward negotiating can be attributed to a little book called *Getting to Yes*, by Roger Fisher, William Ury, and Bruce Patton.

The "win/win" negotiation approach has these positive attributes:

➤ It de-emphasizes personalities in favor of emphasizing the issues. In other words, it separates the person from the problem.

➤ It focuses on common concerns rather than on stated demands.

➤ It is often based on establishing fair standards for all parties. (If all parties use mutually agreed upon or accepted external standards, the discussions are referred to as *principled negotiation*.)

➤ Its focus on finding common ground means that both sides can come away winners.

Win-Win: An Example

Jody and Bob supervise two separate work teams. New company procedures mean that they have to restructure the way their teams work together. They start by agreeing that they have a common goal: using the new procedures as effectively as possible. Then, they make a list of all the changes they think they will each need, and start looking first at areas that are common ground and high priority for both of them, and work from there. In other words, they are acting as partners in the process, aiming at a win-win solution.

Note here an example of a win-win negotiation approach you've experienced or might experience in your work or personal life:

_____

_____

The Give/Get Principle of Negotiation

The collaborative, or win-win, approach to negotiation is usually the most effective and most rewarding for both parties. However, there will be certain situations you will confront where the concept of compromise, or give-get, fits better.

For many people these days, the word *compromise* has a negative meaning. For others, it describes the necessary give and take of everyday living. Most people feel it is not possible to get something for nothing—there always seems to be a cost or concession made to receive what they want.

In reality, though, the word *compromise* simply means making and/or receiving concessions. In the illustration that follows, you'll see how this give-get principle of negotiation works.

The "Give/Get" Compromise Approach to Negotiation

	Party A	Party B
FORMULA 1	Give/Get	Give/Get
Both parties are willing to give something in order to get what they want, and they enter the negotiation with that plan in mind. How much, and when they compromise are the details to be worked out. This formula has the most potential for success.		
FORMULA 2	Give/Get	Get/Give
Formula 2 also has a good chance of success because both sides understand that a good settlement requires both giving and getting. One party is willing to give providing something comes back in return. The other party will give after having received. The difficulty in this formula is that the getter may decide to see how much can be gotten without giving in return. If the getter goes too far, or waits too long to reciprocate, the giver may decide to revoke concessions previously made and the parties may reach a stalemate.		
FORMULA 3	Get/Give	Get/Give
In this formula, both parties come into a negotiation with the idea they will give nothing until they receive. They will stalemate quickly and remain there unless one party is willing to risk giving in order to get. If neither party budges, there is no negotiation.		

Give/Get: An Example

Let's go back to the example we used for the win-win approach, where Jody and Bob are working out the ways that new procedures will affect how their teams work together. While they are able to find common ground for many of the changes they have to make, they come to some changes which simply can't be worked out that way.

Bob offers to take on the full responsibility for one type of workflow, if Jody will no longer expect that Bob's team handles the incoming mail for both teams. For another process, Jody says she can give up the extra time her team had to do the work, if Bob's will take on added quality control for that process. Bob knows that's not an even exchange of time, but he's willing to compromise (i.e., give to get) on this point.

Note here an example of give-get compromise that you have experienced or might experience in your work or personal life:

_____

_____

Managing Conflict During Negotiation

Effective negotiators do not always get all they want even in a successful negotiation. But they do work hard to get what they need. Each negotiator wants to get as much as she can, yet each knows a compromise may be necessary, and that original goals may have to be altered. Often, meeting the needs of both parties results in a win/win outcome.

Good negotiators always look for ways to convert divergent ideas into channels of mutual interest, or common ground. They emphasize and build on matters they can agree on and avoid dwelling on points of difference.

Still, conflict is often part of negotiation, and you will negotiate more effectively if you understand what causes conflict and learn some effective approaches to managing it.

Causes of Conflict

Conflict in a negotiation may be minor, or it may be a monumental block to achieving success for the parties involved. The parties may mean well, but each is trying to achieve what he perceives to be the best objective for his side of the discussion.

Conflict is present because of:

➤ Differences in needs, objectives, and values

➤ Differences in perceiving motives, words, actions and situations

➤ Differing expectations of outcomes—favorable vs. unfavorable

➤ Unwillingness to work through issues

➤ Unwillingness to collaborate or compromise

Conflict Can Be Healthy or Unhealthy

Conflict becomes unhealthy when negotiators avoid it or approach it only on a win/lose basis.

When this happens, animosities will develop, communications will break down, trust and mutual support will deteriorate, and hostilities will result. The damage is usually difficult (sometimes impossible) to repair.

Conflict is healthy when it causes negotiators to explore.

Negotiators explore new ideas, test their positions and beliefs, and stretch their imaginations. When conflict is dealt with constructively, the negotiators may be stimulated to greater creativity, which should lead to a wider variety of alternatives and better results.

Conflict Resolution Styles

There are five basic approaches to conflict resolution. This chart gives you a handy summary. Indicate the one you are most likely to use in a negotiation.

Style	Characteristic	User Justification
❏ Avoidance	Non-confrontational. Ignores or passes over issues. Denies issues are a problem. May be unable to engage due to physical or mental limitations.	Differences too minor or too great to resolve. Attempts might damage relationships or create even greater problems. Unwilling or unable to confront the issues.
❏ Accommodating	Agreeable, non-assertive behavior. Cooperative even at the expense of personal goals.	Not worth risking damage to relationships or general disharmony. Perceives a payoff by totally giving in.
❏ Win/Lose	Confrontational, assertive and aggressive. Must win at any cost.	Survival of the fittest. Must prove superiority. Seen as most ethically or professionally correct.
❏ Compromising	Important all parties achieve some goals and maintain a relationship. Aggressive, yet somewhat cooperative.	No one person or idea is perfect. There is more than one good way to do anything. You must give to get.
❏ Problem Solving	Needs of both parties are legitimate and important. High respect for mutual support. Assertive and cooperative.	When parties will openly discuss issues, a mutually beneficial solution can be found without anyone making a major concession.

The problem solving style provides the strongest basis for win/win outcomes.

You may find the following diagram helpful in understanding conflict resolution styles.

Assertive	Win/Loss		Problem Solving
		Compromising	
		●	
Unassertive	Avoidance		Accommodating
	Uncooperative → Cooperative		

This diagram is based on the *Thomas-Kilmann Conflict Styles Inventory*.

Conflict Resolution Styles

Answer the following questions:

1. Which style is the most uncooperative and least assertive? _____

2. Which style is characterized by assertive behavior, yet represents the maximum in cooperation? _____

3. Which style is totally cooperative but unassertive? _____

4. Which style is totally assertive and uncooperative? _____

5. Which style takes the middle ground on assertiveness and cooperation? _____

Check your answers in the Appendix.

Did you notice that these styles are similar to the negotiation styles we looked at earlier in this section? The approaches we take to negotiation and conflict are often similar. When we manage conflict, we are taking our approaches and attitudes a step further to resolve conflicts that come up in negotiation. You can learn to use different approaches to become a more effective negotiator.

Now that we have looked at styles, approaches, and attitudes related to negotiation, let's pause to apply all this, looking at the characteristics of the successful negotiator.

Characteristics of a Successful Negotiator

All successful negotiators have certain characteristics in common that increase their chances for favorable outcomes. This is a good time to evaluate your personal characteristics as a negotiator.

Some people do not become good negotiators until they rethink their approach.

Remember also that conflict is normal and is the natural by-product of a challenging negotiation.

The following evaluation can help you determine the potential you already possess and identify characteristics you want to practice and develop. Circle the number that best reflects where you fall on the scale. The higher the number, the more the characteristic describes you. Be honest about how you see yourself. When you have finished, total the numbers circled in the space provided.

1. I am sensitive to the needs of others.	10	9	8	7	6	5	4	3	2	1
2. I am committed to a win/win philosophy.	10	9	8	7	6	5	4	3	2	1
3. I am a good listener.	10	9	8	7	6	5	4	3	2	1
4. I am willing to research and analyze issues fully.	10	9	8	7	6	5	4	3	2	1
5. I have a high tolerance for conflict.	10	9	8	7	6	5	4	3	2	1
6. Patience is one of my strong points.	10	9	8	7	6	5	4	3	2	1
7. My tolerance for stress is high.	10	9	8	7	6	5	4	3	2	1
8. Personal attack and ridicule do not unduly bother me.	10	9	8	7	6	5	4	3	2	1
9. I understand the distinction between "wants" and "needs."	10	9	8	7	6	5	4	3	2	1
10. While I like to win, I am willing to compromise to solve problems when that appears necessary.	10	9	8	7	6	5	4	3	2	1

GRAND TOTAL_____

Evaluating Your Results

If you scored 80 or above, you already have many characteristics of a good negotiator. You recognize what negotiating requires and are probably willing to apply yourself accordingly.

You may want to choose a couple of areas to further develop for yourself.

If you scored between 60 and 79, you can do well as a negotiator, but have some characteristics that need further development. Choose those that seem most important to you to develop.

If your evaluation is below 60, you should go over the items again carefully. You may have been too hard on yourself, or you may have identified some important key areas on which to concentrate as you negotiate. You can use this evaluation and this book as a guide to developing your skills.

You may repeat this evaluation after you finish this book, and again after you have had practice negotiating, to see if your score changes.

Case Study: A Buy-Sell Negotiation

Whenever negotiation involves either a purchase or a sale, the temptation is great to approach the transaction from a win-lose perspective. As you go through this case study, notice the perspectives of the various participants. Notice, also, that, in many cases, a negotiation process can include various styles and approaches as the participants work it out.

Al and Jill's New Boat

Al and his wife, Jill, have recently purchased a small home on an inlet to the ocean. They want a new boat. Their current boat—a 16-foot runabout—has always been used in fresh water. Al and Jill want to be able to stay out overnight, so they feel they need a more substantial saltwater boat. They have been to boat shows, watched ads in the newspaper, and visited boatyards to see what boats were available for sale. They also know they will have to sell their current boat to afford a new one.

Al spotted a nifty 26-foot small cabin cruiser for sale at a boatyard 20 miles from their home. He thinks the price of $15,000 seems fair, considering the age and condition of the boat. The owner likes Al and tells him he'd like to see Al get the boat. Al tells the owner he feels Jill needs to see it before he can make an offer. The owner warns Al that several people have seen the boat and have expressed a serious interest. The owner feels he'll sell the boat that day.

Al finds himself in a difficult position. He likes the boat and feels the final sale price is both fair and affordable. He believes the owner when he says that the boat will sell fast. However, Al feels he owes it to Jill to get her opinion on the boat and the price. And, they have not yet sold their current boat.

Al feels they can get at least $3,000 for their freshwater boat. Jill's co-worker Sam has admired the boat and has told Jill he'd like to buy it if they were ever going to sell it. Jill offers the boat to Sam for $4,000.

Sam offers Jill $2,000 for the freshwater boat, thinking he might get it for a lower price than if he started at $2,500. Jill says no, but says she would accept $3,500 if Sam could pay cash that day, which would help Jill and Al buy their saltwater boat. Sam raises his offer to $2,500. After much bargaining, Jill lowers her price to $3,250 and Sam raises his offer to $2,750. Next, Jill suggests splitting the difference. At this point Sam now has the option of holding firm, splitting the difference, or making a modest increase in his offer to $2,800. This may be a tough choice for Sam. He decides to test Jill's resolve by offering her the $2,800.

When Jill tells Sam she needs $3,000 to be able to buy another boat and Sam tells Jill that he cannot come up with more than $3,000 cash, the deal is struck.

Questions:

1. How would you characterize Al's attitude and approach when he is talking with the boat dealer?

    _____

    _____

    _____

2. How would you characterize the boat dealer's approach, given what little you know of him?

    _____

    _____

    _____

3. In Sam and Jill's negotiation, where do you see an example of win-win negotiation?

    _____

    _____

    _____

4. In Sam and Jill's negotiation, where do you see examples of give/get negotiation?

    _____

    _____

    _____

Compare your answers to the authors' suggestions in the Appendix.

Summary

Here are the main points that were covered in this part. Check those that are most important to you.

- ❏ Our attitudes toward negotiation and conflict are important to consider, because they have a major impact on how effectively we negotiate.

- ❏ The win-win and give/get styles of negotiation are usually the most effective.

- ❏ In any negotiation, it is important to pay attention to our own interests and needs, as well as those of the other party. This allows us to work toward common ground, or to a workable compromise.

- ❏ Practicing ways to manage conflict during negotiation leads to more effective negotiation.

- ❏ Conflict is healthy when it leads to exploration of different approaches; it becomes unhealthy when people try to avoid it or work with only a win-lose approach.

Negotiation:
The Process

Preparing to Negotiate

> **"** *Preparing for a negotiation is a year-round function, as is negotiating."*

—**Gerard Nierenberg,** *Fundamentals of Negotiating*

Preparing for negotiation is as important as the negotiation itself. As you prepare, you have time to think about your needs and wants, about those of the other people involved, and about the style and approach you will take. You also prepare for important details like time and place.

Seven Key Considerations

Effective negotiation preparation includes consideration of the following:

➤ Establishing objectives or goals. What do you want or need?

➤ What do you know about the other person's wants or needs?

➤ What are the positions vs. interests? What is it you would like to see happen vs. what is it you need to see happen?

➤ Who will conduct the negotiation—you or someone else representing you? What about the other person?

➤ Where and when will you meet?

➤ Who will set the agenda?

➤ What ground rules, if any, might be needed?

➤ What homework is required, before the actual negotiation begins?

If all this sounds like work, it is. As with almost everything else in life and work, the extent and completeness of advance planning directly relates to a positive outcome. If time permits, try to set forth (in writing if possible) an outline of your goals and expectations for the negotiation, based on the above list.

Being clear about what you are negotiating, and about the seven considerations outlined above, is essential. A simple checklist like the following one will help.

NEGOTIATION PREPARATION CHECKLIST

Pretend that you are about to negotiate in the following situation:

You work in a nonprofit organization that raises money for children's health issues. Your computers badly need a software upgrade, and you know of several types of software that would fit your needs well, as well as other software that would help even if it didn't do everything you want. It would also be helpful if someone could install the software for you, and maybe even show the staff how to use it.

You will be negotiating with Judy, one of your most generous donors, who also owns a computer store. Since Judy already contributes much to your organization, you understand that she might be hesitant to donate the software outright. You're probably going to have to reach some kind of agreement with her for your organization to pay at least part of the price.

Now complete the checklist that follows as much as possible (it is okay to make up a few things!).

Negotiation Preparation Checklist

With whom am I negotiating?

_____

When?_____Where? _____

Any ground work or homework needed ahead of time?

_____

_____

Now place your wants, needs, and issues in order of importance to you, starting with the most important need and continuing through the least important want at the bottom of your list. By doing this exercise, you will automatically think of alternatives which, in turn, should be ranked.

<u>My Issues</u>   <u>What</u>?   <u>Need</u>?   <u>Alternative</u>?

_____

_____

_____

_____

_____

<u>Other Party's Issues</u>   <u>What</u>?   <u>Need</u>?   <u>Alternative</u>?

_____

_____

_____

_____

As you rank your list for yourself, and you think about what the other side wants or needs, you will be well on the way to finding a possible win-win solution. By being mindful and sensitive to the other side, you practice a collaborative, problem-solving approach rather than an adversarial approach, and you are bound to achieve far more than if you take a hard-line, adversarial, me-vs.-you stance.

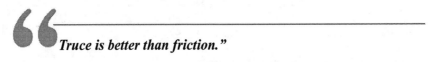

Truce is better than friction."

—**Charles Herguth, quoted in** ***Bits & Pieces***

Compare your answers to the authors' responses in the Appendix. There you will also find a blank checklist to use in future negotiations.

Collecting Detailed Information

> *Clarifying expectations sometimes takes a great deal of courage. It seems easier to act as though differences don't exist and to hope things will work out than it is to face the differences and work together to arrive at a mutually agreeable set of expectations."*

—Stephen Covey, *The Seven Habits of Highly Effective People*

The negotiation preparation checklist you just used will give you all or most of what you need to prepare effectively for simple negotiations. In many cases, however, it will be useful and even critical to get more detailed information before you negotiate.

Here are some guidelines for collecting detailed information. Note that these are similar to the steps we have already looked at; these guidelines expand the material to provide additional information.

- ➤ Describe in detail the issues that are important to you.

- ➤ Identify and rank the interests that must be met for you to be satisfied with the outcome.

- ➤ Describe various settlement options that will meet your needs, satisfy your interests, and resolve the issues.

- ➤ Identify in as much detail as you can the issues you think will be important to the other party or parties involved.

- ➤ Identify and rank the interests that they would like to have met to be satisfied with the outcome.

- ➤ If possible, describe settlement options that you think will meet their needs.

- ➤ Integrate the issues, interests, and options of your side and the other side to determine where common interests and common ground exist, what alternative solutions might be acceptable to all parties, and what differences will have to be overcome.

Negotiator's Guide to Preparation

> ❝ *Preparation does take time, but it probably saves more time than it takes. A well-prepared negotiator can narrow the issues for agreement ... far more quickly and wisely than a negotiator who does not know the terrain.* ❞

—Fisher and Ertel, *Getting Ready to Negotiate*

This multipurpose support tool includes all the concepts involved in preparing for negotiation. You can use it both as a pre-negotiation preparation checklist, as well as for your post-negotiation review.

Using the checklist won't take long for a minor negotiation, and you can't afford to miss anything in a major one.

❑ **1. Define Goals and Objectives**

— Exactly what do I want from this negotiation?

— What do I have to get to meet my needs?

— Am I willing to give up anything to get what I want?

— What are my time and economic requirements for this negotiation?

— What resources will it take to successfully proceed?

❑ **2. Clarify the Issues**

— What are the issues as I see them?

— What is the supporting framework for my position?

— How will I present it to the other party?

— What are the issues as seen by the other party?

— How will they support their position?

— What appear to be the significant differences in the way the parties view the issues?

— Where might the common ground lie?

❑ **3. Gather Information**

— Who will I be negotiating with and what do I know about them? How do they approach a negotiation? What are their needs?

— When and where will the negotiation take place? What advantages or disadvantages do the time and place alternatives have for me? For the other party?

— What are the economic, political, and human implications of the issues?

— What personal power do I have that I can use constructively in this negotiation?

— What power issues must I watch for from the other side?

— What have the past negotiation results been, if known, on issues such as these?

❑ **4. Humanize and Set the Climate**

— How can I best establish rapport with the other party and win his/her trust?

— How can I establish a win/win climate?

❑ **5. Prepare for Conflict**

— What might be the major points of conflict?

— How will I deal with conflict if it occurs?

— How might I determine what the other party needs as compared to what they want?

— Can I handle the negotiation myself or do I need assistance, before, after, or during the negotiation?

❑ **6. Resolution of the Issues/Negotiation Success**

— How will I attempt to resolve conflict? How will I respond to the other party's attempts to resolve conflict?

— What concessions am I prepared to make? Under what conditions?

— What do I expect in return for my concessions?

— Which are my needs and which are my wants?

❑ **7. Agreement and Confirmation**

    — How formal must it be?

    — What approval process will be required? How long will it take?

    — What implementation steps will be needed?

    — Can we ensure peaceful resolution of future issues arising out of this agreement?

PREPARATION SUMMARY

Think before you speak

Look before you leap

Plan before you negotiate

If there is something you wish to acquire through negotiating, be prepared to take a few risks. Good preparation will help you keep risks manageable and provide you with a feeling of confidence.

The Seven Basic Steps in Negotiating

"People, not facts, determine the success of each negotiation."

—**Morrison and Calero,** *The Human Side of Negotiation*

The negotiation process involves specific steps, although they may flow easily into each other. Many texts and handbooks have been written about negotiation. These often contain complex, multilayered steps or action items. However, the following seven simple steps will do very well in carrying out an effective negotiation.

Step 1   Getting to know the negotiators, including yourself

Step 2   Making a statement of goals and objectives

Step 3   Starting the process

Step 4   Revealing disagreement and conflict

Step 5   Ironing out the differences—reducing the negotiating distance

Step 6   Communicating to find alternatives for resolution

Step 7   Reaching agreement in principle, settlement, and acknowledgment

Step 1: Getting to Know the Negotiators

The negotiators include you. If you are wearing a mask, remove it. Negotiating is like any other social situation that has a business purpose. It moves more smoothly when the parties take a little time to get to know one another. It is helpful to assess those involved before negotiations begin.

Of course, it is essential that you know yourself first. Thus, your first question must be: Who am I in this negotiation? Am I the tough fighter, the conciliator, the mom or dad, the businessperson?

Once you have answered that and understand your own motives, approach, and attitude, seek next to know the other person. If you can get information on individual backgrounds, that can provide an excellent guide to importance placed on the issues and the degree of expertise on the subject. As the process starts, you should observe, listen, and learn. A good rule of thumb is to keep the beginning friendly and relaxed, yet businesslike.

Know the Level of Authority

Since agreement is the ultimate objective of any negotiation, it is important to know from the start the level of authority of the party you are negotiating with. In hard bargaining, some sellers will negotiate to know your position, and then they inform you that they do not have the authority to accept your terms. Then they go to some unseen person who will reject any agreements you might make, attempting to leverage a better deal for the seller.

When you have the authority to make an agreement, always strive to negotiate with a person who has the same level of authority.

Now let's ask our friend Sylvia from Widget International to be our guide as we travel through these negotiation steps. As we do so, you'll see questions about your ideas and reactions for each step. These questions have no "right answers"; they are here to help you think about each step for yourself.

Sylvia has been a successful young executive for six years. She has moved steadily up the corporate ladder and now receives a decent salary plus a bonus based on her team's performance. She has had a boyfriend, Peter, for over a year. They plan to marry in two years if all goes well for them. He is finishing law school. Sylvia is ready to buy a townhouse.

Being a thorough researcher, she has studied ads and has even visited several new townhouse projects. Both Peter's and Sylvia's parents have offered to help financially, but Sylvia insists that she has the financial resources to handle the purchase herself. Sylvia has done her homework and has decided which unit she wants to purchase, visited the complex she liked, seen the model townhouses, and met several members of the sales staff.

She has determined she'd like to work with George. She has learned that George has a daughter almost the same age as she is. Sylvia will observe George's attitude and approach to the sale closely. She will watch for clues on how best to talk with him. She will assess both his willingness and authority to bargain as well as his desire to make the sale.

If you were in this situation, what are some of the things you would like to know about George?

_____

_____

_____

Step 2: Stating Goals and Objectives

Remember that you need to find out your own interests or needs so your discussion can be focused on a goal. Ask yourself what success in the negotiation would look like to you.

After the opening, negotiating usually flows into a general statement of goals and objectives by the involved parties. Specific issues might not come up at this time, because the parties are just beginning to explore each other's wants and needs. The person who speaks first on the issues may say, for example, "I would like to ensure this agreement works in a way that benefits everyone concerned." No terms have been suggested yet, but a positive statement has been made about the goals for the outcome.

Positive Communication

Effective communication and active listening are critical at this stage. The person making the opening statement should then wait for feedback from the other party to learn if both parties have similar goals and objectives. If there are differences, now is the time to learn them. The art of effective listening is as important to successful negotiation as the art of effective speaking.

Communication must be a two-way street or it's not communication. If only you speak, it is talking, lecturing, preaching, scolding—but it is not negotiating. As Dr. Stephen Covey notes, highly effective people "seek first to understand, then to be understood."

It is normally a good idea to make the initial statements positive and agreeable. This is no time for hostility or defensiveness. An atmosphere of cooperation and mutual trust is what works best at this stage.

As George takes Sylvia to a townhouse unit just being finished, Sylvia comments, "I hope the unit you are showing me is similar to the model unit I viewed and that the price will be fair." She adds, "I picked this townhouse development because I felt the developers would be able to make a profit while giving buyers a good buy at the same time. Both are important to me."

If you were George, what might you say to state your own objectives for the transaction?

_____

_____

_____

Step 3: Starting the Process

Some negotiations are complex and have many issues to resolve. Others may have only a few. No one can accurately predict the direction negotiations will take until both parties have presented the issues. There may be hidden needs neither party has raised. These will surface as things proceed. In fact, as the process begins, issues that need discussion and possible resolution must come out for the negotiation to be successful.

Combining or Splitting Issues

Often issues are bundled, so the solution to one depends on the solution to another. For example, "I will not agree to buy the pre-owned vehicle at that price, unless a free one-year warranty is included."

On the other hard, there might also be an attempt to separate issues to make them mutually exclusive. For example, in the sale of a furnished house, the seller may prefer to discuss the house and furnishings as separate negotiations. The buyer may feel they should be combined. In some negotiations, all issues are connected. No one issue is considered resolved until all have been resolved.

As noted earlier, a skilled negotiator will study the issues closely before negotiations begin to determine where advantages may lie in splitting or combining issues.

Once the negotiators have reviewed the issues, they must begin dealing with them one by one. Opinions vary about whether to begin with a minor or major issue. Some feel you should start negotiation with a minor issue that has the potential of being easily resolved because this will establish a favorable climate for additional agreements. Others feel it is better if you begin with a major issue, because unless you resolve it satisfactorily, the other issues are unimportant. The attitudes of the parties and their personal styles will determine how the issues will unfold.

George responds to Sylvia's comments by asking exactly what she is looking for in a townhouse regarding size, location, and amenities. He asks her if she has a pre-set price range she can afford and is willing to spend. Sylvia outlines the specifications she hopes will be met and George acknowledges that he is certain they can be satisfied in a unit he is selling. George adds that she is looking for extras, such as a garage, which are expensive and will take her above her expressed price range. Sylvia replies, "I don't see why they should."

If you were Sylvia, how might you feel at this point? Would that change your approach to negotiation, and if so, how?

_____

_____

_____

_____

_____

_____

Step 4: Revealing Disagreement and Conflict

Once the issues have been defined, disagreement and conflict often will occur. This is natural, and you should expect it. Good negotiators never try to avoid this phase because they realize that this process of give and take is where successful deals are often made.

Disagreement and conflict handled properly will eventually bring the negotiators together. If handled poorly, they will widen the differences. Conflict has a way of bringing out different points of view and crystallizing the real wants and needs of the negotiators. Try to look at conflict as normal, even necessary, for clarification.

Wants vs. Needs

When presenting the issues, most negotiators will explain what they want. "Wants" represent positions and are often based on opinions. It is the task of the other negotiator to find out what the person needs, or will find satisfactory. "Needs" represent the resolution minimums and are usually based on data.

Remember that few negotiators get all they want, but good negotiators will work to get as much as possible. They understand that give and take may be necessary and that they might need to modify their goals. Here is where your attitude and approach are most important. As noted earlier, approaching the negotiation with a view toward satisfying needs, rather than toward "I win; you lose," creates far greater potential for success.

When opposing wants are revealed, it can feel like confrontation. This confrontation can involve stress. It is important to remember, therefore, that conflict resolution under these circumstances is not a test of power but an opportunity to reveal what people need. Understanding this leads to discovering areas where you can agree or collaborate. Try to think of conflict as opportunity.

Sylvia picks the model she wants and asks the price. George responds, "$149,000." Sylvia is surprised and disappointed, since she thought the asking price was advertised as $125,000. She expresses this to George. The unit Sylvia has picked, notes George, has a number of features, including a garage, which were not part of the advertised unit. Sylvia acknowledges this, but is still upset and wonders if George is putting something over on her.

If you were George, what might you think you will need to pay more attention to at this point? What could you say to Sylvia to show you are aware of what this conflict means to her?

_____

_____

_____

Step 5: Narrowing the Gap Between Negotiators

Most parties want to resolve differences, especially when something is at stake for them. This is especially true when negotiating. At some point, normally one party will move toward common ground. Flexibility, within limits, is a powerful tool in negotiation. A good negotiator can develop several possibilities that will yield a good result.

Statements reflecting willingness to test the waters or send up a trial balloon in the discussions will often begin with phrases like, "Suppose that …?" "What if …?" or "How would you feel about...?" When these statements begin, you should listen carefully to see if they indicate an offer to attempt resolution.

Then your response should be carefully stated. Too quick an attempt to pin something down may cause the other party to withdraw because the climate may not seem conducive to giving and getting. If both sides begin to see a way that the solution can be win-win, they can reduce the negotiating distance, often fairly quickly. This requires each of you to evaluate the options and then select the one that works best for you while also allowing the other side to win something (i.e., meet their minimum needs).

"Echo" Responses

When you respond to offers, it is a good practice to state them back. As noted in Step 2, feedback creates more effective communication, and more effective communication increases the chances for negotiation success.

Suppose an automobile salesman tells you that he will sell you a car for $750 less than the sticker price. You could respond to him: "You will sell me this vehicle, as is, for $750 less than the sticker price?" This type of response has at least three advantages:

➤ You might get an improved offer because the seller may get the impression your echo is a negative response to his offer.

➤ The seller may attempt to justify the price. This will provide opportunities for challenge, clarification, and further bargaining.

➤ Your echo will also give you time to think about a counteroffer.

Remember, however, that if you make an offer that is critical to you, and the other negotiator echoes it, you should simply confirm your offer, not sweeten it. Your confirmation forces the other negotiator to accept it, reject it, or suggest an alternative.

Sylvia tells George she needs time to think about George's last statement. She says, "I just can't pay that much. I'll have to try to find a unit elsewhere." George offers a unit with fewer features, but Sylvia stands firm. After a pause, George asks Sylvia if she could handle $139,000. Sylvia replies, "$139,000?" George then adds, "That includes the garage." Sylvia answers, "I can't exceed $130,000."

Can you think of other statements George might make to Sylvia to try to iron out the differences, given that Sylvia feels so strongly at this point?

_____

_____

_____

Step 6: Finding Alternatives for Resolution

Sometimes eliminating substantial gaps in the negotiating distance between the parties requires new thinking. In mediation, this is called the "problem solving" or "brainstorming" step. You can use the same tools a mediator uses to help bring parties closer to the common ground by "unfixing" your position. It may mean stepping out of a hard-bargaining (win-lose) model to a more collaborative and creative (win-win) approach.

Finding the acceptable alternative requires effective communication. Both parties must communicate their ideas and positions in a way that leads to receiving and understanding. You can communicate effectively only when you learn to listen effectively.

Also, be aware that when you listen, you are not necessarily hearing what is being said, but rather what your own filter tells you is being said. By feeding back what you think you hear, you increase dramatically the chances for successful communication and can convey that to the other party.

Sometimes, you can find a successful alternative if one or both parties look for additional information or get an expert opinion.

George asks Sylvia if she has to have a garage. Sylvia responds that she wants her car protected from the weather. George informs her that carports are available to provide some protection for vehicles at far less cost than enclosed garages. Sylvia then asks George for the lowest recent selling price on a unit comparable to the one she wanted, but with a carport. George goes to the office and returns with records of the three most recent townhouse sales for units such as the one Sylvia desires.

What do you think Sylvia and George have each decided at this point?

_____

_____

_____

Step 7: Agreement in Principle, Settlement, and Acknowledgment

When agreement is reached, you will need to affirm it. You will need a decision about how the final settlement will be obtained, especially if additional approval is required. This normally means placing the agreed-upon terms in writing. If possible, this should happen while the parties are together so they can agree on the language. Reducing the agreement in principle to some form of writing will reduce the danger of a misunderstanding later.

George shows Sylvia the information on the other sales and responds to Sylvia's offer of $130,000 by saying, "I just can't sell that unit for $130,000, but if you will accept a carport instead of a garage, I will let you have it for $135,000." Sylvia replies, "If that includes closing costs, you have a deal."

Are there other alternatives you would be satisfied with if you were Sylvia?

_____

_____

_____

The agreement and resolution will have far greater effect and positive influence on relationships if, after the deal is struck, the parties acknowledge each other and the good work they both did. Remember the "scorched earth" or "Attila the Hun" negotiator can never go back and pick up the pieces.

Sylvia thanks George for the way he handled the negotiation. George tells Sylvia that he sincerely appreciated working with her and that if she ever needs anything for her new home, she could call on him. She knows that she now has a good contact at the town house complex if she should have a problem.

After the Agreement Is Reached

Two additional important considerations for the negotiator are acceptance time and the post negotiation review.

Sometimes, things don't happen as quickly as we might like. This is especially true in negotiation.

As you go through the negotiating process, be ever mindful of the need for acceptance time. A negotiation often forces people to face something new or different for them. People need time to accept anything new or different.

Parties enter negotiations hoping to get what they want quickly and easily. This is not always possible. Sometimes people make incorrect assumptions, or they may have some misconceptions about the facts being discussed. Readjustments or new approaches might be needed. These take time. As with other aspects of negotiation, you will find that continued creativity and approaches based on win-win or collaboration with be most effective.

Post-Negotiation Review

It is always a good idea to do some type of analysis following each negotiation.

You can do this in writing or as a mental exercise. Doing the review will help you determine reasons for your success or failure and will give you valuable information in future negotiations. In your review, examine the strengths and weaknesses of your opponent's approach as well as your own. Think about what worked and what did not. Think about what motivated you and what motivated the other side.

The Negotiator's Guide to Preparation presented earlier is an excellent guide and tool for your post-negotiation review. Once you have done your review, file it away for reference before your next negotiation.

Reviewing the Seven Basic Steps in Negotiating

Following is a brief summary of the seven steps common to each negotiation. Keep these in mind before you engage in your next negotiation.

Step 1   Know yourself and who you will be at the negotiation. Be sincere. Get to know the other party. Keep initial interaction friendly, relaxed, and businesslike.

Step 2   Share your goals and objectives with the other party. At the same time, learn their goals and objectives. Work to create an atmosphere of cooperation and mutual trust.

Step 3   Start dealing with the issues one by one. Be prepared for this by studying the issues before the negotiations begin to determine your advantages in splitting or combining issues. During negotiation, also pay attention to how the other person is bringing up issues.

Step 4   Once the issues have been defined, express areas of disagreement or conflict, and listen to the other parties' conflicts as well. It is possible to resolve the differences in a way that is acceptable to both parties only when conflicts are out in the open and examined.

Step 5   Reassess positions. Determine where the common ground might be, and what level of compromise might be acceptable. If you must compromise, remember the give-get principle.

Step 6   Once positions are clear and the common ground is discovered, be flexible within reason, and look for alternative approaches that might help resolve remaining issues.

Step 7   Both parties affirm any agreements that have been reached. Insure there is no misunderstanding later by placing the agreements in writing (when possible), and sharing them with the other side. Remember that mutual agreement is the ultimate objective of any negotiation.

This is a good time to take a moment to reflect on what you have read.

Completing the exercise on the following page will help stimulate your thinking.

READING REVIEW

Circle the most appropriate choice for completing each of the statements below.

1. In negotiating, it is beneficial to:

    A. Take a little time to get to know the other party

    B. Get down to serious business immediately

2. Step 2 of a negotiation gives the parties:

    A. A chance to challenge each others position

    B. An opportunity to express objectives

3. Collaboration is a sign that:

    A. One side has won and the other has lost

    B. Both sides have used a problem-solving approach

4. Compromising in a negotiation:

    A. Is a sign of weakness

    B. May be necessary to get what you need

5. As issues are being clarified, it sometimes:

    A. Appears the differences are irreconcilable

    B. Becomes apparent that some issues are closely tied to each other

6. When conflict occurs in a negotiation, you should:

    A. Work toward its constructive solution

    B. Go to a less controversial item

7. When a negotiator says, "What if I were to install…?"

    A. The reassessment and compromise step has begun

    B. The negotiator is showing weakness

CONTINUED

8. It is a good idea to:

   A. Learn the authority of the person you are dealing with in advance

   B. Assume the other person's level of authority is the same as yours

9. Winning the negotiation:

   A. Is possible when common ground is discovered

   B. Is not possible unless the other side loses

10. The courage and confidence necessary to start a negotiation:

   A. Are inborn

   B. Come with a willingness to learn skills and prepare

Check your answers in the Appendix.

Summary

Here are the important concepts that were covered in this section. Check those that are most important to you.

- ❑ Effective negotiation requires careful preparation. When you are well-prepared, you can go into negotiation more confidently.

- ❑ To prepare well for negotiation, get together as much information as possible about your goals, your needs and wants, and your possible alternatives.

- ❑ Prepare similar information about the other party as well as you can. This will help you move toward a win-win solution.

- ❑ Remember to plan the details of time and place, and ask other people to help or speak for you if needed.

- ❑ The negotiation process has seven steps that move from preparation, through revealing objectives and conflicts, toward resolution and agreements.

- ❑ In the negotiation process, it is important to be aware of what is going on for the other party, so that you can work toward common ground as much as possible.

- ❑ Often, as you move through the seven steps of negotiation, you will find that the negotiation requires a combination of approaches. Frequently, you will use a combination of win-win and give-get.

- ❑ In a conflict, or in the discussion of offers during a negotiation, it is sometimes helpful to "echo" what the other person has said. This provides added time for reflection, clarification, and reconsideration.

- ❑ When you have concluded a negotiation, remember to consider the need for acceptance time and post-negotiation review.

P A R T 4

Strategies and Tactics

Negotiating Through Give to Get

Negotiators soon learn that for the negotiation process to be successful, both sides have to feel comfortable with the result. Most times, an honest, fair, win-win approach works best. But sometimes in negotiation, you have to give in order to get. These are the two approaches emphasized in this book: collaboration (win-win) and compromise (give-get).

The real skill in using the give-get approach is the ability to determine what to give, when to give, why to give, how much to give, and what to expect in return. To become an expert negotiator, you have to know how to maneuver, so that if you have to give to get, what you give you both can afford, and what you get will satisfy your needs.

The strategies and tactics in this section are specialized tools you can use as added methods to maneuver through the give-get approach, or to give yourself other approaches when collaboration and compromise aren't working for you.

➤ A strategy is the overall plan of action employed in a negotiation

➤ Tactics are the step-by-step methods used to implement the strategy

Using a business analogy, you can think of a strategy as the business's overall plan for the year. Tactics are the actual processes and tasks the company will use to make the plan work. In the examples here, the strategies are the concepts, and the tactics are the actual words and other methods of communication the negotiators use.

You will see these strategies and tactics in action in the sections that follow as they apply to the negotiations for Tom and Gerry's new office:

Tom and Gerry have decided to completely remodel and update their office space. Their first choice is to work with a local office furniture and design company that does work they really like and that would suit their needs—but information on the designer's Web site shows what they want at $200,000, which is about $20,000 above their limit. Tom feels, however, that the results would be excellent for their business, and that they should make an offer to the designer. Gerry doubts they could get the price down enough to make a difference.

Tom decides to do some further research and learns that because an out-of-town discount office-furniture place is offering similar designs at a lower price, their local designer's business has slowed down. Tom convinces Gerry they have nothing to lose by making an offer. After some careful planning, they make an appointment to see a salesperson for the local designer they like.

Five Basic Strategies in Action

Negotiators often use one or more of five basic strategies, which are:

- ➤ Lowball
- ➤ Pinpoint the need
- ➤ Challenge
- ➤ Defer
- ➤ Split the difference

You will probably recognize some of them in the examples that follow. See how Tom and Gerry use each of these strategies as they negotiate for design fees on their office remodel.

APPROACH	STRATEGY
Tom and Gerry describe to the salesperson what they want to do, saying they really like the work they have seen from this designer. Tom says that they really might be sincerely interested in going forward at a lower price, such as $160,000.	**LOWBALL**—They are going for the lowest possible price for what they want. They are trying to buy at what they estimate the designer's costs might be and what they think is the lowest possible price they might succeed with.
The salesperson sounds shocked and says, "That's impossible; we wouldn't even consider it!" Tom and Gerry had anticipated this response, and ask, "If $160,000 won't work for you, what will you take?"	**PINPOINT THE NEED**—With their lowball offer, Tom and Gerry have established that the designer will take less than the $200,000 price, but not $160,000. The task now is to pinpoint how much less than $200,000 the designer needs.

APPROACH	STRATEGY

The salesperson does some figuring before he says, "$190,000, but we do have advance payment requirements, and you would need to advance us at least $40,000." Tom and Gerry had hoped for a lower counteroffer, but were prepared for the $190,000 response. Gerry tries another strategy by saying, "The advance payment is no problem, but I've talked to a couple of businesses where you've done similar work at something like $25,000 less than the asking price. Why won't you do the same for us?"

CHALLENGE—This is a strategy designed to put the other party on the defensive in an effort to win some concessions. Gerry knows he has to use it carefully, but he has some information to back him up. Added to Pinpointing, this helps to determine what the seller will actually take.

The salesperson reacts by saying, "Those were probably long-term customers, and we had more latitude to do what we wanted. But perhaps I could trim the price a bit more, say, to $185,000, if we could do the initial paperwork today, and you could provide the $40,000 advance within 10 days." Tom and Gerry, sensing they are close to their goal, reply, "We really do like your company's work, but it is still more than we want to pay. Please excuse us while we discuss ways in which we might increase our offer. Would you please reevaluate your position too?"

DEFER—Tom and Gerry take a break to allow themselves and the seller time to reevaluate their positions. Deferring a decision for reconsideration and recalculation often proves that patience pays.

Gerry and Tom return in an hour and offer $170,000. The salesperson tells them: "I've talked with my manager while you were away to see if further concessions were possible. He gave a little, but $170,000 just won't do. However, if you would be willing to split the difference, and make it $177,500, we can make a deal, providing you can do the paperwork today and provide your advance within 10 days." Tom and Gerry look at each other and accept with smiles on their faces.

SPLIT THE DIFFERENCE—Tom and Gerry carefully calculate their counteroffer in hopes the seller will either accept the offer or suggest Splitting the Difference. The result is a sales price at the midpoint between the seller's last offer and Tom and Gerry's counter proposal.

It may seem as if there was a compromise in Tom and Gerry's office deal because the give/get approach resulted in positive benefits to both parties. Although this negotiation began as win-lose (Tom and Gerry wanted to get the better of the deal than the designer), it ended up as a win-win. By changing from lowball (a more confrontational approach) to pinpointing the need (a more collaborative approach), the result was a deal in which both parties got what they needed.

Identifying Other Negotiation Strategies

There are many other negotiation strategies and tactics. The ones identified in this section can get a bit more complicated, but can also be very effective. You can gradually add strategies like these to your negotiation skills.

As you'll see, these strategies are sometimes used manipulatively and even dishonestly. Always bear in mind the basic goal of win-win or give-get for successful negotiation.

Salami

Salami is a technique used to achieve an objective a little bit at a time rather than in one giant step. This strategy is said to have been named by Matyas Rakosis, general secretary of the Hungarian Communist Party, who explained it in this way:

"When you want to get hold of a salami that your opponents are strenuously defending, you must not grab at it. You must start by carving yourself a very thin slice. The owner of the salami will hardly notice it, or at least he will not mind very much. The next day you will carve another slice, and then still another. And so, little by little, the salami will pass into your possession."

Example

Let's say, you want to buy five acres of land from someone who simply cannot decide to go ahead with such a large sale. As you talk, you realize the person would be fine going through with a smaller sale. You are in no hurry to acquire all five acres at once. You could offer to buy one acre now, then either negotiate a timetable to buy the others one at a time, or simply wait till the person is more open to selling.

Fait Accompli

Fait accompli comes from the French for "It's already done." In this strategy, the person completes one phase of a project, or does a lot of work before conditions are negotiated, hoping that the other party will be willing to go ahead because so much work is already done. As you'll see in the examples, this strategy can be a risk: if it doesn't work, you've wasted time and effort, and perhaps money.

Example

You really want to be the person chosen from your department to work on a specific project team. So, before asking Bill, your manager, to choose you, you put a lot of time and effort into researching the project and writing out your suggestions. Then you give it to Bill, hoping that he will be impressed by your work and choose you—and he does!

In this next example, the strategy is used manipulatively and illegally:

Residents of a community called Riverview woke up one morning to discover a local developer removing a beautiful, historic stone fence across the road from their development. The fence was an appealing part of their view. The developer did not have a legally required permit, but once removed and taken apart, that fence could not be restored. He hoped for acceptance—but may well end up with a lawsuit instead.

Standard Practice

This strategy is used to convince others to do or not to do something because of "standard practices" (also sometimes referred to as "industry standard"). It often works well because it implies it is the best way to do whatever needs to be done. At times, those standards actually cannot be changed, and the negotiators have to look at other areas to negotiate instead. Sometimes, though, the standard is not an unchangeable rule and can be negotiated.

Example

Standard (or "boilerplate") contracts are an example of this strategy. The party suggesting a standard contract assumes no one would want to change it, because it reflects what others routinely agree to under the circumstances. Often the other party will accept the contract as a fact of life, but those who wish to test it can have good results.

Then again, some standards, like some building safety codes, cannot be changed or negotiated. For example, building codes today include accommodations for the disabled that must be built into new construction. So if you were negotiating costs for a commercial building, you would have to find other areas that could be cut to lower costs.

Deadlines

Time is critical to people and organizations. Consequently, deadlines can be an effective negotiation strategy. All too often we are aware of time pressures on ourselves, but assume the other party has plenty of time. A better assumption would be that if we have deadlines, the other party probably has them too.

The more we learn about the other party's deadlines, as well as our own, the better we can plan our own strategies. When others attempt to force us to their deadlines, we should not hesitate to test them. Deadlines are usually as demanding as we are willing to think they are. Be careful, though. Sometimes the deadline is fixed, and you can lose a deal or opportunity for failure to comply with a solidly fixed deadline.

Example

Some sales in retail stores that "start" on Tuesday and "end" on Friday can be negotiated so a buyer can take advantage of them on a Monday or Saturday as well. Many hotels will extend their checkout time beyond noon if you are willing to negotiate for a later time. Proposals requested by the first of the month are often just as acceptable on the second.

Deadlines often play a part in business negotiations. If you are managing a project, for example, you usually have multiple deadlines to establish and meet. It's important to be sure those deadlines are well-negotiated as the plans take shape, to help avoid problems later on.

Feinting or Trial Balloons

The feint or trial balloon is an attempt to test the other party's priorities, or to test acceptability before making a final decision. Good negotiators send up trial balloons at various stages of negotiation. The other party's reaction gives a good sense of what will fly and what won't. If the other party reacts favorably, or at least has little or no opposition to what you are saying, then you can usually proceed to another step or level of discussion.

Example

An employee who wants an increase in salary may start negotiating with the boss for a promotion. If the promotion is forthcoming, so is the raise. If the promotion is not possible, but the boss does not seem negative about the person's performance, the employee may then be able to negotiate a raise on another basis. Community officials use a variation of this strategy to test receptivity by the public to something they plan to do. They publish a concept or a plan and evaluate the public's response. If there is little opposition it is probably safe, in the official's mind, to proceed to the next step. If there is an adverse reaction, the official may try another approach.

Apparent Withdrawal

This strategy combines deferring, feinting, and sometimes deadlines. You use it to indicate to the other negotiator that you will withdraw from consideration of an issue if your terms are not met. Its purpose may be to ultimately get a concession or change in position. You are sending up a trail balloon to see how the other negotiator will react when you propose leaving instead of completing the negotiation.

This strategy also can have some high-stakes risk. By leaving with a view toward returning to get a better deal, you may risk losing the opportunity to obtain what you want. Or, other circumstances might come up before you have time to return, and someone else may end up getting what you want.

Example

The prospective buyer of an antique dresser finds the seller unwilling to meet the price the buyer is prepared to pay. The buyer might say, "I'm sorry, but I'm not willing to meet your price. You know my price, so unless there is some movement on your part, we can't do business." The buyer then leaves. If the buyer has made a realistic offer, the seller may decide to make a concession. If not, the buyer can always go back with a slightly higher offer. In the meantime, of course, the buyer can consider other options. And, if someone else who likes the unique piece comes along in the meantime, willing to pay the seller's asking price, the first buyer loses the piece.

Good Guy/Bad Guy

The good guy/bad guy ploy is a widely recognized strategy. Usually, it is used when two negotiators are working as a team opposite another negotiator or team. One member of a negotiating team takes a hard-line approach while another member is friendly and easy to deal with. The good guy and the bad guy sometimes take turns leaving the room, so the other party deals with one approach or the other alone. Some individual negotiators use this strategy alone, switching back and forth between the good-guy and bad-guy roles.

Problems can arise with this strategy. The other party may recognize exactly what is happening, and may start playing it as well. This strategy can also lead to lack of trust, or to win-lose results. On the other hand, there may be a real need both to be friendly and to take a hard line in the context of a negotiation. The key is in knowing what you really need and working toward that goal.

Example

Anyone who has seen a police or spy film or watched "cop dramas" on television will be familiar with this strategy. In everyday life, there are many more examples, and often less adversarial examples, of this strategy. Salespeople, lawyers, spouses, personnel representatives, accountants, tax experts, supervisors, managers, and co-workers regularly use it, sometimes effectively, sometimes not.

Limited Authority

Limited authority is an attempt to force acceptance of a position by claiming any other deal would require higher approval. Individuals who claim to have limited authority are difficult to negotiate with because they say that the reason they cannot meet your demands is someone else, some policy, or some practice over which they have no control.

You have a choice of how to respond to this strategy. You might concede under these circumstances. Or, you might question the truth of the "limited authority" or insist that your offer be taken wherever necessary for approval or rejection. There is some risk this will terminate the negotiation, but it does give the other party a chance to gracefully reevaluate their position.

It's important not to confuse this strategy with what might be a reality: sometimes it is true that one negotiator actually will propose something the other negotiator has no authority over.

Example

Some salespeople use this approach, claiming they cannot give more than a 5% cash discount, or can't influence the delivery date. Work teams sometimes use this when group planning doesn't go as hoped. They talk about having to go back to managers to get authority to go further. Occasionally, people use this strategy even though they can make the decision themselves, because they want the added issue of authority to come into play.

DO YOU RECOGNIZE THESE STRATEGIES?

Draw a line to match the strategy in the left-hand column with the description or example in the right-hand column.

(a) Lowball

1. This is a good way to approach a complex situation with many parts.

(b) Pinpoint the need

2. "Sorry, we always do it this way; we have to use these steps in the process."

(c) Defer

3. You have a $1,000 difference between your offer and the other party's. You decide you can go halfway, offering $500.

(d) Split the difference

4. You tell the other party you need time to think and will come back the next day.

(e) Salami

5. This means starting with a small offer to see if the other party will accept it or if you need to offer more.

(f) Fait Accompli

6. The other party says that your answer is needed by 5 P.M. that day, no later.

(g) Standard practice

7. "Well, I can't give you all that information to complete the project without asking my supervisor first."

(h) Deadlines

8. The other party starts talking about leaving if you don't meet some specific conditions.

(i) Feinting/ trial balloon

9. As a team leader, you send out a plan before a negotiation with another department, just to see how they react.

(j) Apparent withdrawal

10. "Just how long can you give me to complete this project?"

(k) Good guy/ bad guy

11. A salesperson approaches you with "a package I already put together for you, all the work done ahead of time, you just have to agree and sign."

(l) Limited authority

12. You find yourself facing a negotiator who seems to be switching back and forth between being friendly and somewhat difficult, so you realize you need to work harder to bring the discussion back to some point of common ground.

Check your answers in the Appendix.

Ten Critical Mistakes to Avoid

Now that you have learned some helpful strategies, let's think about the critical mistakes negotiators sometimes make. To reach your maximum potential as a negotiator, you must make every effort to avoid them.

1. **Inadequate preparation**

   Preparation provides a good picture of your options and allows for planned flexibility at the crunch points.

2. **Ignoring the give/get principle**

   Each party needs to conclude the negotiation feeling something has been gained.

3. **Use of intimidating behavior**

   Research shows the tougher the tactics, the tougher the resistance. Persuasiveness, not dominance, makes for a more effective outcome.

4. **Impatience**

   Give ideas and proposals time to work. Don't rush things; patience pays.

5. **Loss of temper**

   Strong negative emotions are a deterrent to developing a cooperative environment, and to creating solutions.

6. **Talking too much and listening too little**

   Effective listening is a powerful tool in working toward better understanding and a collaborative solution.

7. **Arguing instead of influencing**

   You can explain your position best with education and information, not with stubbornness.

8. **Ignoring conflict**

   Conflict is the substance of negotiation. Learn to accept it and resolve it, not avoid it.

9. **Failing to be creative**

   It's best to enter every negotiation with possible alternatives to call upon if necessary

10. **Missing the areas of common ground**

    Even in the most adverse negotiations, there are places where you will both agree. Be prepared to build upon these. Big agreements are often built upon small agreements.

Summary

Here are the important concepts that were covered in this section. Check the ones that are most important to you.

- ❑ You can learn a variety of strategies and tactics to use in negotiation.

- ❑ It is important to learn how to choose the strategies and tactics that will be both appropriate and effective for each negotiation.

- ❑ To learn a strategy well, think about examples of how you might use it and practice it before you go into negotiation.

- ❑ You can become a stronger negotiator by learning to recognize the strategies the other party is using.

- ❑ Remember that the ultimate goal of any strategy is a successful negotiation. Always keep in mind the win-win and give-get approaches.

- ❑ Watch out for critical mistakes; they happen most often when you forget to prepare, when you forget your basic goal, or when you show emotions that are too strong.

Developing
Your Skills

Case Study: Negotiating a Project Plan

Team projects are a good place to watch negotiation at work and to use your negotiation skills. Although the project itself is usually not set up as a negotiation, areas needing negotiation almost always come up in any project.

The following case study will give you a chance to put together many of the basic concepts for effective negotiation. You may want to complete the whole case study before checking your answers in the Appendix, or you may check yourself for each answer as you go along.

Rewriting a Procedures Manual

Bob, Joan, Diane, and Steve have been asked to work as a team on a project to rewrite a procedures manual that is outdated. Bob and Joan are from the sales department; Diane and Steve are from the customer service department.

Those departments are the main users of the manual, but tech support and the shipping department also use it as a reference when they work with either sales or service on certain tasks. Other departments also use it occasionally.

Bob, Diane, and Steve have good negotiating skills and have worked regularly in situations requiring negotiation. Joan knows the basic concepts of negotiation, but this will be her first experience in a project that will require considerable negotiation in several areas. Also, she has been with the company only a couple of months.

Steve has been chosen to be the project lead. He knows that this process will require a lot of negotiation on a number of topics because of the variety of needs and wants represented in this project. He approaches this with the idea that his task is to lead the group through a win-win process. He is also aware that there are one or two sections of the manual that are the source of repeated conflict between the two departments, and that there are people who feel very strongly about their positions in these areas.

The main task of the project team is to develop a process to rewrite the manual, and then to oversee the rewriting and implementation.

Preparation

Before their first meeting as a project team, Steve sends out a checklist of the information he thinks is important for them to use to prepare for that first meeting. Gathering this information will help all of them prepare for negotiations, and will help with their project planning as well. His list includes the following:

➤ What are the main issues their two departments have with the manual?

➤ How do they see each other's issues with the manual?

➤ What issues can they find out that other users have with the manual?

➤ Who are all the various users who have any interest at all in the manual?

➤ What are the main areas that will need revision work?

➤ How long do they think the process will take, or, how much time do they really have to get it done?

➤ How does the printing and publication process happen in their company?

➤ Will the new manual be online instead of a paper manual?

➤ What are each team member's specific goals for the process they will set up?

➤ Who will be responsible for which aspects of the process?

Your Turn

1. What additional information do you think would be useful for the team members to put together before their first meeting?

   _____

   _____

   _____

   _____

   _____

The First Meeting

Steve opens the meeting by thanking the others for the work he knows they have already done in preparation for the meeting. He thanks them for coming to the meeting and particularly welcomes Joan, since this is her first participation in a team project since she joined the company. He mentions that he's glad they can all work together to a common goal.

Steve says that, to tackle this project effectively, they perhaps should start by listing all the major issues and needs to consider, and then create their plan with those in mind. The conversation then goes something like this:

Bob: Well, I came across an important issue when I talked to tech support. They wanted to know who was going to have the final authority on the manual. They said they didn't want to have it. They realized it wasn't their manual, but they wanted to know, and they also wanted to have some review authority before publication.

Diane: Well, hasn't it always been sort of "our" manual? I mean, in customer service we have way more procedures than you people do in sales. And we know a lot about what customers need and want and the problems they run into.

Bob: But if it weren't for sales, you wouldn't have customers to work with in the first place! I think we really are "in charge" here.

Joan: Well, where I came from, each manager who had someone in a project had to sign off on it before we did any implementation. Is that the way you do it here? It seems to me like we're all talking about customers anyway. When I was in training last month, they told me that my job in sales is to bring in the customers, and service has the job of keeping them. Umm … sorry, hope I haven't jumped in too much here.

Steve: That's OK, Joan. I think you've got a good point when you mention that it's all about the customers anyway. That's the whole point of the procedures in this manual.

Diane: Well, I think I can agree on having both our managers do the "official" signing off on it. I just want to be sure that customer service gets what we need, especially when it comes to how we follow-up after we've talked with a customer.

Bob: Yes, I think I'd be fine with both managers equally signing off on it—we may have to work harder to get that consensus but I think it's worth it. I just don't want sales procedures to get ignored, especially when it comes to how we hand off customers to service.

Your Turn

2. Can you identify what has happened in this exchange, related to approaches and styles of negotiation?

   _____

   _____

   _____

3. What was the major issue here, and why is it so important in any negotiation?

   _____

   _____

   _____

4. If you were on this team, where do you think you might use the win-win approach, and where might you use the give/get approach?

   _____

   _____

   _____

Compare your answers to the authors' suggestions in the Appendix.

Analysis

Of course, the work of this team will go on much longer and will include several meetings and further negotiations. Their first negotiation, however, shows promise of a successful process. They have been willing to deal with conflict, and they have reminded themselves of their common ground.

Negotiations that happen in a larger context, such as project work, can be more complex. There are more people and more issues involved. In this case, conflict has not come up within an individual department yet, but there is a good chance that at some point it could come up.

This case illustrates how negotiation often comes up in daily work, in daily life. It's important to recognize it and to remember that effective negotiation principles and approaches are the key to success, regardless of the scope or complexity of the process.

MEASURE YOUR PROGRESS

It is time now to review the progress you have made. On the line to the left of
each statement, write T if the statement is true and F for false.

_____   1. Negotiating skills can be learned but they require consistent
practice.

_____   2. Good negotiators are willing to research and analyze issues
carefully.

_____   3. Negotiating is one area in which patience is not a virtue.

_____   4. Advance planning is not possible in negotiating.

_____   5. Successful negotiators stress winning at any cost.

_____   6. Too much advance preparation reduces your flexibility.

_____   7. Compromise is a tool used by weak negotiators to save face.

_____   8. Conflict is an important part of any negotiation.

_____   9. People need to be given time to accept changes and new ideas.

_____   10. Always do a "post negotiation analysis" to improve your learning
from the experience.

_____   11. Most of the information we need prior to a negotiation can be
obtained by asking questions and doing some basic research.

_____   12. The more authority you have, the better when negotiating.

_____   13. Your objectives for every negotiation should be well thought out.

_____   14. Negotiators should be well versed in the techniques of conflict
resolution.

_____   15. Your expectation level has a direct relationship to what you achieve
in a negotiation.

_____   16. Anytime we attempt to influence another person through an
exchange of ideas, or something of material value, we are
negotiating.

CONTINUED

5: Developing Your Skills

_____ 17. It is possible for both parties to win in a negotiation because everyone has different needs and wants.

_____ 18. Looking for the common ground is a basic rule of successful negotiating.

_____ 19. Competition for what you have whether it is money, ideas or products is a source of power.

_____ 20. This book is a great start to build negotiating skills but it should be followed with additional reading, training, practice and advice from experienced negotiators.

Check your answers in the Appendix. Total correct: _____

Each correct answer is worth five points. Your total score: _____

If your score was 80 or better, you've acquired the basic concepts necessary to become, with practice, an excellent negotiator. If your score is below 80, give yourself some added review: re-read parts or all of this book and then retake the test if you wish.

Either way, remember that good negotiators are "made, not born." You can use this book as a reference any time you want to review and add to your skills as a negotiator.

Applying What You Have Learned

Reflect for a moment on what you have been learning, and then develop a personal action plan using the following guide to apply what you have learned.

Think over the material you have read, the self-analysis questionnaires, the case studies, and the reinforcement exercises.

What did you learn about negotiating?

_____

_____

_____

What did you learn about yourself?

_____

_____

_____

How can you apply what you have learned to your personal life?

_____

_____

_____

_____

Your business life?

_____

_____

_____

_____

Your community life?

_____

_____

_____

_____

Make a commitment to become a better negotiator. Use the personal action plan that follows to help you accomplish this goal.

MY PERSONAL ACTION PLAN

Name: _____ Date: _____

1. I am reasonably confident that my current negotiating skills are effective in the following areas:

❑ Identifying and expressing my own objectives, needs, and wants

❑ Identifying and listening to the objectives, needs, and wants of the other party

❑ Researching and preparing information that will help me negotiate effectively

❑ Planning ahead for my possible alternative solutions or areas where I can compromise

❑ Preparing background information on the other party as much as possible

❑ Preparing for the setup of negotiation: who, when, where

❑ Beginning a negotiation with an atmosphere of trust and willingness to move to solutions

❑ Recognizing and handling conflicts effectively as they come up

❑ Using a variety of strategies effectively to move the negotiation along and get results

❑ Finding common ground and moving toward a win-win solution as much as possible

❑ Using the give-get approach when needed to come to a workable compromise without losing the negotiation

❑ Following up after negotiations to insure that agreements get carried out, and to review the process

CONTINUED

CONTINUED

2. I know I need to improve my negotiating skills in the following areas:

- ❑ Identifying and expressing my own objectives, needs, and wants

- ❑ Identifying and listening to the objectives, needs, and wants of the other party

- ❑ Researching and preparing information that will help me negotiate effectively

- ❑ Planning ahead for my possible alternative solutions or areas where I can compromise

- ❑ Preparing background information on the other party as much as possible

- ❑ Preparing for the setup of negotiation: who, when, where

- ❑ Beginning a negotiation with an atmosphere of trust and willingness to move to solutions

- ❑ Recognizing and handling conflicts effectively as they come up

- ❑ Using a variety of strategies effectively to move the negotiation along and get results

- ❑ Finding common ground and moving toward a win-win solution as much as possible

- ❑ Using the give-get approach when needed to come to a workable compromise without losing the negotiation

- ❑ Following up after negotiations to insure that agreements get carried out, and to review the process

CONTINUED

3. My goals for negotiating skills improvement are as follows:
   (Be sure your goals are specific, attainable and measurable.)

   _____

   _____

   _____

   _____

   _____

4. These people and resources can help me accomplish my goals:

   _____

   _____

   _____

   _____

   _____

5. These are my action steps and timetable to accomplish my goals:

   _____

   _____

   _____

   _____

   _____

Congratulations on the good work you've done in completing this course, and good luck in building your negotiation skills.

A P P E N D I X

Negotiation Preparation Checklist

See "The Negotiation Preparation Checklist" exercise earlier in this book for suggestions on using this checklist. This added copy of the checklist is here for you to use for preparing future negotiations.

Negotiation Preparation Checklist

With whom am I negotiating?

_____

When?_____Where? _____

Any ground work or homework needed ahead of time?

_____

_____

Now place your wants, needs, and issues in order of importance to you, starting with the most important need and continuing through the least important want at the bottom of your list. By doing this exercise, you will automatically think of alternatives which, in turn, should be ranked.

My Issues	What?	Need?	Alternative?

Other Party's Issues	What?	Need?	Alternative?

Appendix to Part 2

Comments and Suggested Responses

Conflict Resolution Styles

1. The most uncooperative and least assertive style is **avoidance**. Avoiders are unwilling or unable to engage.

2. The style characterized by assertive behavior, yet representing maximum cooperation is **problem solving**.

3. The style that is totally cooperative but unassertive is **accommodating**. Accommodators see "losing" as their goal.

4. The style that is totally assertive and uncooperative is **win/lose**.

5. The style that takes the middle ground on assertiveness and cooperation is **compromising**. Some people see compromise as "lose-lose."

Case Study: A Buy-Sell Negotiation

1. In one sense, Al's approach can be seen as win-win: he wants to buy the boat, and the dealer wants to sell it to him. However, Al is in some ways looking at win-lose: he realizes he may lose the chance to buy the boat, but he has a key interest that he wants to keep (win): he insists that Jill be part of the decision.

2. The boat dealer seems to be using a win-lose approach: buy the boat today (I win) or it might be gone (you lose). Note that he offers no compromises such as allowing more time for Al to do what he needs to do.

3. Sam and Jill's first negotiation is win-win because it has common ground: both are working toward the purchase of the boat, and they are willing to negotiate to get there.

4. Sam and Jill's later negotiation is give/get as they work out the actual price of the boat.

Appendix to Part 3

Comments and Suggested Responses

Negotiation Preparation Checklist

You will be negotiating with Judy, of course. You may want to have another person from your office there too, if that person can help with the discussion. Judy may also wish to have one of her sales reps with her.

As for when and where: You will want to pick a time that works well for both you and Judy, a time of day when you and she are not too busy, if that's possible. You want to meet in a space that allows you to talk with a minimum of distraction and interruption; if either of you has a quiet office space, that would be best.

Your wants, needs, alternatives: You need software that will do the job for you. You want the best for your situation, if that's possible. You are willing to look at various types. Perhaps you can also be somewhat flexible on when you actually get the software. And it would be so nice to find someone who could install it and show you how to use it.

Judy's needs, wants, alternatives: Thinking about Judy, you realize that she probably would like very much to have her already generous contributions recognized. You know she probably has either a need or a want to have your organization pay for some of the software; you will have to work toward an amount that will work for her (i.e., meet her needs—not wants). You also think that, to provide you an added benefit even if you have to pay for the software, she might be able to have one of her staff install it for you, and may be able to suggest someone who would be willing to provide training.

Reading Review

1. (A) Getting to know the other party helps create an atmosphere of trust and openness.

2. (B) The purpose of Step 2 is to lay out goals and objectives.

3. (B) Collaboration is a win-win approach.

4. (B) Compromise is part of the give-get approach.

5. (B) Clarification helps develop better understanding of the issues.

6. (A) Don't avoid confrontation; aim at working through it to a solution.

7. (A) This kind of offer provides a possible step to a give-get solution.

8. (A) You want to negotiate with a person who has enough authority to give you what you are seeking.

9. (B) A win-win solution based on common ground is the best possible outcome of negotiation.

10. (B) With added learning and practice, you can become a skilled negotiator.

Appendix to Part 4

Comments and Suggested Responses

Do You Recognize These Strategies?

1. (e) The salami strategy means breaking up a process into smaller, more attainable goals.

2. (g) Standard practice is a way to try to keep the other party within limits. The limits may or may not be negotiable.

3. (d) By offering to go with half of the difference, you provide a way to move the negotiation along.

4. (c) Deferring gives both parties a chance to think and reconsider.

5. (a) You use the lowball approach to find a baseline to start from.

6. (h) The other party is attempting to conclude the negotiation by setting a deadline.

7. (l) The other party is using limited authority to push to a conclusion; it may or may not be a reality.

8. (j) The other party is attempting to see how you will react to the withdrawal.

9. (i) You are sending up a "trial balloon" to see how people will react.

10. (b) You are trying to pinpoint the other person's need.

11. (f) This person is trying to get you to agree quickly to work already done, with little or no negotiation.

12. (k) You are dealing with someone who is playing both the good guy and bad guy roles.

Appendix to Part 5

Comments and Suggested Responses

Case Study: Negotiating a Project Plan

1. You might have added budget information, information on how much authority the team has, comparison with other similar manuals in the company, or any other information you think would be useful if you were in this situation.

2. Here are some things you might have noticed: Conflict, on who is really in charge, surfaced fairly quickly. The various comments show that this is an area where there are strong feelings, and people might hold on strongly to some positions. Joan provides a couple of ideas that help: she offers a practical idea on the sign-off, and she brings up the area of common ground that they all need to focus on.

   At that point, even though team members still feel strongly about their positions, they begin offering more specific issues that can lead to specific solutions.

3. The major point of conflict here is one of authority. Remember that naming authority can be used as a strategy to push negotiation in one direction or another. In some cases, however, like this one, there are real authority issues. Apparently, the team members had not thought of checking on this before their meeting. Even if they had, strong feelings might still surface and they might want to have more say in what happens.

4. You might want to keep in mind and remind the others occasionally that the basic common ground is working with customers, and all groups "win" if improved procedures make for better customer relations. When it comes to specific procedures, however, you will probably want to make some give-get agreements, because the two departments do have different types of work, and some compromise will probably be needed.

101

Measure Your Progress

1. True — Practice makes perfect—just ask anyone who has negotiation experience.

2. True — An essential effort.

3. False — Patience and fortitude are musts. Also, a little bit of assertiveness doesn't hurt.

4. False — Planning is one of the secrets of success. Foreknowledge and preparation are keys to negotiation success.

5. False — Successful negotiators believe both parties can win.

6. False — Advance preparation enables flexibility.

7. False — Compromise (give to get) is an important method of conflict resolution.

8. True — When there is no disagreement (conflict), there is no need to negotiate.

9. True — Adequate acceptance time should be an integral part of the plan.

10. True — Learn from your own experience.

11. True — Pretty obvious—the more you know, the better.

12. False — Sometimes, too much authority can lead to a settlement before all the options have been tested.

13. True — You must know what you want to achieve (i.e, what needs must be met). Otherwise, you are wasting time and much effort.

14. True — Negotiation is about preventing or resolving conflict.

15. True — Those who expect little, achieve little.

16. True — This is an ideal result of negotiation.

17. True — If we weren't individuals with our own wants and needs, no one would ever need to negotiate.

18. True — Finding the "common ground," if possible, leads to the best outcomes.

19. True — An especially great power source when linked with tolerance, creativity, and patience.

20. True — Review this book before any negotiation. Also, seek advice elsewhere. The resources are many. A number of solid resources are listed in the Additional Reading list.

Appendix

Additional Reading

Babcock, Linda and Sara Laschever. *Women Don't Ask: Negotiation and the Gender Divide.* Princeton, NJ: Princeton University Press, 2003.

Bonet, Diana. *The Business of Listening.* Boston, MA: Thomson Learning/NETg, 2001.

Decker, Bert. *The Art of Communicating.* Boston, MA: Thomson Learning/NETg, 1996.

Fisher, Roger and Scott Brown. *Getting Together: Building Relationships As We Negotiate.* NY: Penguin Books, 1989.

Fisher, Roger, William Ury, and Bruce Patton. *Getting to Yes: Negotiating Agreement Without Giving In.* NY: Penguin Books, 1991.

Hathaway, Patti. *Giving and Receiving Feedback.* Boston, MA: Thomson Learning/NETg, 1998.

Haynes, Marion E. *Project Management.* Boston, MA: Thomson Learning/NETg, 2002.

Kindler, Herbert S. *Managing Disagreement Constructively.* Boston, MA: Thomson Learning/NETg, 1996.

Lickson, Charles P. *Ironing It Out: Seven Simple Steps to Resolving Conflict.* Boston, MA: Thomson Learning/NETg, 1996.

Lloyd, Sam R. *Developing Positive Assertiveness.* Boston, MA: Thomson Learning/NETg, 2002.

Morrison, Terri, Wayne A. Conaway, and George A. Borden. *Kiss, Bow, or Shake Hands: How to Do Business in Sixty Countries.* Avon, MA: B. Adams Publishing, 1995.

Stone, Douglas, Bruce Patton, Sheila Heen, and Roger Fisher. *Difficult Conversations: How to Discuss What Matters Most.* NY: Penguin Books, 2000.

Ury, William. *Getting Past No: Negotiating Your Way From Confrontation to Cooperation.* NY: Bantam Books, 1993.

Various authors. *Dealing with Difficult People.* Boston, MA: Harvard Business School, 2005.

The quotes used in this book are from the valuable resources noted in the text.

Additional Suggested Resources

Web Resources

If you look up negotiation using any good search engine, you'll get a wide range of resources. Pay attention to the type of information offered: Is it someone advertising their services? Does the site provide you with good usable information? Does the information go with your style and your approach to negotiation?

As with any information search, it is important to note the sources of the information. Is it a website connected to a university or other organization with solid research credentials?

You may also email the author at clickson@cmc-resolution.com

People Who Can Provide Professional Assistance

1. People you know and trust. This might include attorneys, business professionals, counselors, clergy, family, or friends, depending on the topic of negotiation. This kind of support can be very helpful; it's most effective when the person understands the principles of negotiation and the value of the win-win approach.

2. Community resources. In some communities now, there are negotiation and mediation organizations. Before you use their resources, be sure to get plenty of information on who they are, how they work, and their basic approach. Always check to see if their approach is based on common ground, compromise, or win-lose.

3. Professionals such as mediators and facilitators. These are people who have the training to assist in negotiations and mediations. It's important to get a lot of information on their background, approach, and experience.

IMPORTANT NOTE:

In using any of the resources listed, be certain to be clear first to yourself and then with your assistant (if using another person) as to what your negotiation goal is. Are you negotiating to win (and if the other has to lose) or are you looking at how you can both win.

Now Available From

THOMSON
NETg

Books • Videos • CD-ROMs • Computer-Based Training Products

If you enjoyed this book, we have great news for you. There are
more than 200 books available in the *Crisp Fifty-Minute™ Series*.
For more information contact

NETg
25 Thomson Place
Boston, MA 02210
1-800-442-7477
www.courseilt.com

Subject Areas Include:

Management

Human Resources

Communication Skills

Personal Development

Sales/Marketing

Finance

Coaching and Mentoring

Customer Service/Quality

Small Business and Entrepreneurship

Training

Life Planning

Writing